We Are Kids Too

The Adventures of Danny and Emily

KAREN BLESSINGTON

PHOTOGRAPHS BY DAVID GARMAN

 FriesenPress

Suite 300 - 990 Fort St
Victoria, BC, v8v 3K2
Canada

www.friesenpress.com

ISBN
978-1-4602-8891-7 (Hardcover)
978-1-4602-8795-8 (Paperback)
978-1-4602-8796-5 (eBook)

1. JUVENILE NONFICTION, ANIMALS, HORSES

Distributed to the trade by The Ingram Book Company

This book is dedicated to Schuyler Helford and Aven Helford, my two legged kids that continue to inspire me from many miles away. To their dad, Bruce Helford, whom I will never be able to thank enough for his kindness over the years.

I would like to thank Pat and Athene Voisey for saving wee Emily. Since their invaluable advice came at a critical time in young Emily's life, I have a happy healthy filly that otherwise may not be here now.

Finally, to the McLeod brothers, Norman and Colin. Norman, you are the most courageous person Dave and I have ever known. Keep up the good work, young man! Colin, you are the best little brother in the whole world. Your dedication and love is a true inspiration to us.

Hello. My name is Danny. This is a photo of my mum

and I when I was only a year and a half old. A baby boy

horse is called a colt.

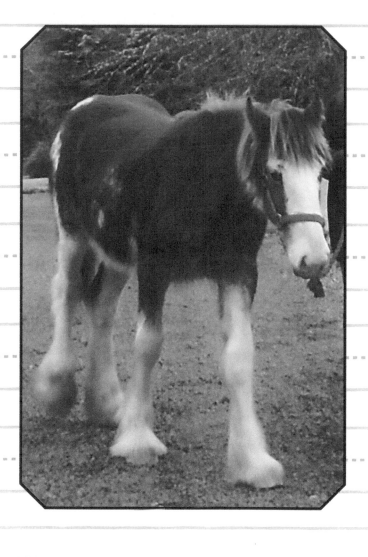

I'm Emily. I am a wee baby girl of 10 months here.

A baby girl horse is called a filly. Danny and I are

brother and sister.

We are Clydesdale horses. We will get to be very

big and strong when we grow up. Our family comes

from the Clyde Valley in Scotland.

One day we got to go for a ride in a big truck. When

the truck stopped, we were at our new home! There

were people to greet us. We were scared, but the

people were kind and made us feel welcomed.

At our new home, there was a nice house built just

for us. Home sweet home.

After our long journey, we were very hungry. Being

growing babies, we need to eat a lot so we can grow

big and strong.

Traveling and eating made us very tired. We had to

lay down for a nap. Because we are kids too, we need

our sleep.

When we woke up from our nap, we were ready to

play. Mud puddles are great fun, but . . .

. . . our favourite game is Clydesdale catch! We have

a big ball that is a lot of FUN!

Because we are kids too, we like to play on swings

just like **YOU.**

We also like to play Clydesdale hide and seek. See

how good I am at hiding? Emily never did find me.

Now we're 3 and 4 years old. We love each other

very much. We spend a lot of time mutual grooming

each other. This is how we show affection to one

another. It feels nice.

Because we are kids too, sometimes we get scared

of things like walking across a rickety bridge.

But when we got across it, we felt very proud

because we were brave enough to try.

Just like you, we grow fast. We need to get our

hooves trimmed on a regular basis because they grow

really quick. It doesn't hurt. It's just like getting

your fingernails trimmed.

Because we are kids too, we are curious about things

in our world. This red rubber boat was interesting

to us.

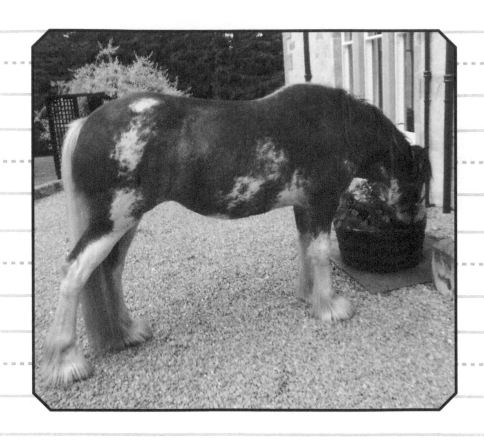

Because we are kids too, sometimes we are naughty

and get into trouble. Like this time when wee Emily

got scolded for eating the pretty flowers. But they

tasted so good. Mmmmm. . . flowers!

We have a lot of friends that don't look like us. This

is T-Bone. She is a Highland Cow. T-Bone is usually

shy until we say hi to each other.

These are our neighbours. They are Highland Ponies

called Squeaky and Poppy. Squeaky makes funny

sounds like she swallowed a dog toy.

Our other neighbours are the sheep. They eat a grass

mixture called haylage in the winter when there isn't

enough grass for everyone. Sometimes the sheep

share with us. They are thoughtful and giving.

Harry the Harris Hawk

is quite the silly bird. He squawks loudly and makes

himself look big by spreading his wings. After awhile,

though, Harry became our friend once he realized

we wouldn't hurt him.

This is Sparky the dog. She is still afraid of us

because we are so much bigger than she is. One day

we hope to play with her.

Because we are kids too, we go to school to learn

how to work when we are older. Our classroom is

outside and we love to learn. In this lesson, we are

learning long reining. It teaches us which direction

to go when we are pulling a heavy load.

I am a working draft horse. That means that I pull

cut logs out of the forest. At the end of my busy

day, I always like to check out my hard work!

Because we are kids too, we lose our baby teeth. As

we get older, our teeth continue to grow because

when we chew our food we wear them down.

Because we are kids too, we like to take good selfies.

Danny told me that there is a snowman in here
somewhere. I think he may have been teasing me. Big
brothers do that sometimes.

Emily told me that there is a pot of gold at the end

of this rainbow. I think she may have been teasing

me. Little sisters do that sometimes.

Because we are kids too,

we are a lot like you.

We love to run and play.

We learn something new every day.

The time has come to say goodbye.

It's all good, friend. Do not cry.

Danny and Emily will soon be back

With more adventures to keep you on track!

To be continued. . .